Wonders of the World

Acknowledgments

Executive Editor: Diane Sharpe
Supervising Editor: Stephanie Muller
Design Manager: Sharon Golden
Page Design: Rafi Mohamed
Photography: Bruce Coleman: pages 14-15, 17, 21; Robert Harding: cover (top right, bottom right); Popperfoto: page 26; Science Photo Library: pages 28-29; Tony Stone: cover (middle right), pages 9, 10, 12-13, 19, 22-23, 25.

Library of Congress Cataloging-in-Publication Data

Hunphrey, Paul, 1952-
   Wonders of the World?/Paul Humphrey; illustrated by Lynne Willey.
      p.   cm. — (Read all about it)
   Includes index.
   ISBN 0-8114-5733-8 Hardcover
   ISBN 0-8114-3790-6 Softcover
   1. Landforms — Juvenile literature.   2. Natural monuments — Juvenile literature.   [1. Landforms.   2. Natural monuments.]   I. Willey, Lynne, ill.   II. Title.   III. Series: Read all about it (Austin, Tex.)
   GB406.H86   1995
   551.4'1—dc20

                                                                    94-28181
                                                                        CIP
                                                                         AC

1 2 3 4 5 6 7 8 9 0 PO 00 99 98 97 96 95 94

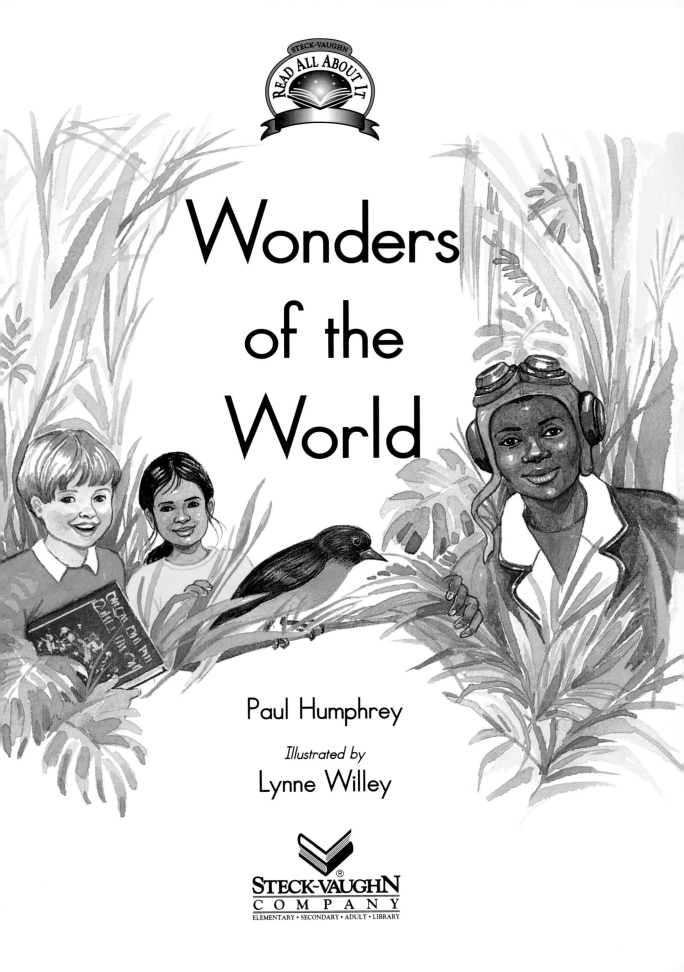

Wonders of the World

Paul Humphrey

Illustrated by
Lynne Willey

STECK-VAUGHN
C O M P A N Y
ELEMENTARY · SECONDARY · ADULT · LIBRARY

4

The geyser called Old Faithful spouts out hot water in a huge fountain every 30 to 120 minutes.

The water in geysers comes from deep inside the earth where it is very hot.

The Grand Canyon in Arizona is about one mile deep. The canyon was formed by the Colorado River cutting through the rock.

The Iguaçú Falls are between Brazil and Argentina. They are almost three miles wide.

The world's highest waterfalls are in Venezuela, which is also in South America. They are called the Angel Falls and are over 3,000 feet high.

There are volcanoes all over the world. The hot, melted rock pouring out of a volcano is called lava.

The Great Barrier Reef is off the coast of Australia. It is made up of billions of corals. Corals are tiny animals with hard skeletons.

Ayers Rock is over one mile long and about 1,000 feet high. It is a holy place for the native people of Australia. They call the rock Uluru.

Now we are in the rain forests of Indonesia.

It is very hot and damp here.

Listen to the noises of the animals and birds.

Rain forests are home to thousands of different plants and animals.

20

Many of the world's rain forests are
in danger. People must stop cutting
them down.

Mount Everest is over five miles high.
It is in a range of mountains called
the Himalayas.

24

An oasis is a water hole in the
desert. Palm trees can grow there.
People often live around an oasis
and farm the land.

They are called the Northern Lights.
The glowing lights often make strange
shapes in the sky. Sometimes they look
like rippling curtains or searchlights.

Cheddar Caves are full of stalactites and stalagmites. Stalactites hang down from the cave ceiling, and stalagmites grow up from the cave floor.

They make funny shapes.

They look like giant icicles.

How many wonders of the world that
we visited can you find on the map?
The answers are on the last page, but
don't look until you try naming everything.

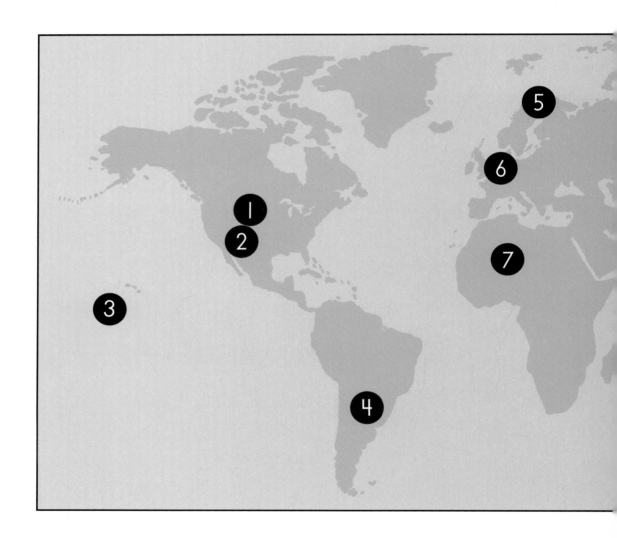

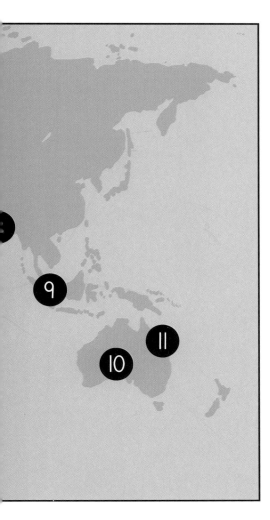

Index

Answers: 1. Old Faithful 2. Grand Canyon 3. Hawaiian volcanoes
4. Iguaçú Falls 5. Northern Lights in Norway 6. Cheddar Caves
7. Sahara Desert 8. Mount Everest 9. Indonesian rain forest
10. Ayers Rock 11. Great Barrier Reef